FREE YOURSELF

Simene' Walden

FREE YOURSELF by Simene' Walden
Published by The Student Teacher

P.O. Box 813

SAVAGE, MD 20763

www.simenewalden.com

© 2017 by Simené Walden

All rights reserved. Copyright under Berne Copyright Convention, Universal Copyright Convention, and Pan-American Copyright Convention. No part of this book may be reproduced, stored in a retrieval system, or transmitted in any form, or by any means, electronic, mechanical, photocopying, recording or otherwise, without prior permission of the author.

For permission contact:

thestudentteacher17@gmail.com

Editor: The Student Teacher

First Printing, January 23, 2018

Printed in the United States of America

ISBN: 978-0-9997987-5-1

If you are interested in special quantity discounts for bulk purchases please contact the author directly via email.

Table of Contents

Additional Books by The Author vi

About the Author vii

Testimonials from "Standing On His Words: Prayers and Devotionals Every Educator Can Pray" ix

Standing On His Words Courses and Seminars xii

Testimonials from "Spiritual Combat" xvii

Spiritual Combat Workshop xviii

Speaker Topics xix

Simene' Walden's Signature Message 1

Free Yourself in Your Thinking 2

Free From Your Family 50

Free Yourself From People 75

Free You From Your Self 133

Additional Books by The Author

Standing On His Words Ebook Available

@ bit.ly/2Stand

Standing On His Works Print Book Available

@ bit.ly/2StandBook

Standing On His Words Action Guide Available

@ bit.ly/StandingWB

Spiritual Combat Print Book Available

@ bit.ly/combatprayerbook

Spiritual Combat EBook Available

@ bit.ly/combatprayer

My Heart Under A Microscope Available

@ bit.ly/heartunderscope

The Student Teacher Quotes Available

@ bit.ly/studentteacherquotes

For booking inquiries and speaking engagements, please contact the author @ <u>thestudentteacher17@gmail.com.</u>

About the Author

A native of North Carolina, Simene' (Sim ma nae) Walden grew up in Northampton County, North Carolina where she attended Northampton County Public Schools. During the initial five years after graduating high school, she pursued her education at three different colleges only to find herself back where she started: Fayetteville State University. In 2004, Simené graduated with a Bachelor of Arts degree in English & Literature from Fayetteville State University. Ten years later, she obtained her Masters of Arts degree in Christian Studies with an emphasis on Youth Ministry from Grand Canyon University.

Simené also known as "The Student Teacher", was given that name by the Holy Ghost on June 7, 2016. She is a teacher by vocation but is always in a place of learning something new that will catapult her to the next level in her destiny. Simene' is a teacher, accountability coach, writer, speaker, and an Amazon Best Selling Author. She believes in being teachable and remains in a posture of learning even from those one may not think has anything to offer. Simene' believes that everyone has something to offer. Simené's primary objective is to empower, educate, and equip others as she teaches them everything she has learned.

She actively serves in various ministries in her local church. God's servant openly shares her love for God on her social media sites as well as in the marketplace. Her ministry started on the streets of Washington, DC. She is the Chief Operating Officer of *The Student Teacher*, where she is flooding the Educational System with God's Words of prayer. Simene' is also the author of Standing On His Words: Prayers and Devotions Every Educator Can Pray, Standing On His Words Workbook: Prayers and Devotions Every Educator Can Pray, Spiritual Combat, and My Heart Under A Microscope. Her sixth book Youth In Crisis will be released in January.

Contact the author:

thestudentteacher17@gmail.com

www.simenewalden.com

https://www.facebook.com/thestudenteacher

https://www.twitter.com/@simenewalden

https://www.periscope.tv/@simenewalden

https://instagram.com/simenewalden

Mailing Address: P.O. Box 813 Savage, MD 20763

Testimonials from
"Standing On His Words: Prayers and Devotionals Every Educator Can Pray"

Recently, I purchased, Standing on His Words, by Simene' Walden because I was interested in learning about how I could spiritually address many of the challenges within the educational system. From the first prayer, Empowering Educators Through Prayer, I was captivated by the power and passion that was outlined as she exposes the devil in schools across the world! Each prayer addresses the reasons why prayer is important for all of us regardless of whether we are educators, administrators, or parents. As an administrator, there is a prayer that directly speaks to preparing my heart to address the needs of my schools in a professional Christ-like way as opposed to the way of the world. My favorite is chapter called, Prayers for Intercessors Praying for the Educational System. This chapter is call to action for all people to confront the specific challenges close to their hearts and intercede through prayer. As a mother, I have prayed several devotions from this book over my child daily, and I am looking forward to using it in conjunction with my Bible as there is specific scripture that that accompanies each devotion. I cannot wait to see the manifestation of God's power through these prayers! Thank you, Simene' for writing this book to encourage us as adults to pray for our children and ourselves to be better stewards over the God's Kingdom. I stand with you in the movement of #praying4schools through #StandingonHisWords.

(Alma, Amazon Review)

Both as an advocate for Moms in Prayer, an Educator and a mom myself, I find this resource to be invaluable! The power of prayer is monumental and we need it now more than ever! Excellent guide!

(Anita, Amazon Review)

As an educator, I recommend this book to my fellow educator as a reminder of why we do what we do. Get your copy today!

(Aikyna, Amazon Review)

This book is one to not only Read BUT keep out ON your desk!! Soooo many great insights and prayers for sooo many at different stages AND struggles as well!! GREAT reference!!! A Definite book to get for all!!!!!

(Kelly, Amazon Review)

It is good you are sharing your gift with the world, and educators in particular. I haven't read a book on this topic yet. Thanks again.

(Deborah, Colleague)

Standing On His Words Courses and Seminars

Young Adults (17-24)

The Struggle Is Real: Parents Just Don't Understand

Do you often bump heads with your teenager and/or young adult? Do they feel like they are always being corrected for doing something wrong that they actually believe is right? Do they seem lost and frustrated because they want to create the life God has for them, but they have no idea what that is and what that looks like?

If you answered yes to either of these questions, this seminar is for your child!

This seminar will give your child real-solutions to very real problems in a very real and aggressive world. Within this workshop, teenagers and young adults will learn how to perfect the areas of concern in their lives from biblical truths and practical teaching.

The four modules will include the following:

1. How to create a blueprint for your life?
2. How to take the opinions of others and learn from them?
3. How to talk to God and get real-time answers?
4. How to focus on yourself and become the Best YOU?

Adults (25-40)

The Struggle Is Real: People Just Don't Understand

Do you often bump heads with people? Are you criticized about the way you see things and how you live your life? Do you often feel like the people around you do not relate to you and don't understand your viewpoint on many things?

This seminar will give you real-solutions to your very real problems in a very real and aggressive world. In this class, you will learn how to perfect the areas of concern in your life from biblical truths and practical teaching.

The four modules will include the following:

1. How to create a blueprint for your life?
2. How to take the opinions of others and learn from them?
3. How to talk to God and get real-time answers?
4. How to focus on yourself and become the Best YOU?

(Educators, Leaders, Administrators)

Creating a Culture of Collaboration and Respect

As the demands of excellence, production, and results are eminent, do you desire to respect all children regardless of their behaviors and interactions with you? Do you wish to respect and gain respect from fellow colleagues? Do you work in an atmosphere that could use some positive TLC?

In this class, you will learn how to create a place of peace in the environments that seem to be dominated by drama, negativity, and hostility.

The six modules will include the following:

1. How to create a culturally sensitive and affirmative environment?
2. How to create an Educational Environment not mirrored by the image of the Penal System?
3. How to protect yourself from being influenced by the accusations of others?
4. How to minimize distractions in the workforce?
5. How to honestly communicate with others even when angry?

Additional Seminars and Courses Include:

How to avoid "burn out"?

How to have the heart of a teacher and not just the knowledge of one?

Each seminar and course is a 4-hour session that includes the book and all other materials.

For booking inquiries and speaking engagements, please contact the author directly via email @thestudentteacher17@gmail.com.

Testimonials from "Spiritual Combat"

This book gave me more scriptures to read for my healing and how to fight my enemies. This is a very good read.

(Victoria, Amazon Review)

This is a phenomenal read that will equip you for battle in the spirit realm. This book should be in every Christian soldier's arsenal!

(Brent & Angel Rhodes - Marriage of God, Amazon Review)

Spiritual Combat Workshop

Prayer Board

Does your life look like you envisioned it? Is your life aligning with what a parent, pastor, or prophet has told you? Has the Word failed you or have you failed the Word? Do you even know what the Word says about your situation and your life?

In this class, you will learn how to create the life you want by designing a visual prayer board of your necessities, needs, and desires from God. In this course, you will learn how to apply God's Words to your prayer request to obtain God driven and God given results.

The six modules will include the following:

1. Identifying your necessities, needs, and desires.
2. Finding scripture that answers your prayer request.
3. Gathering pictures that align with your prayer request.
4. Designing your prayer board.
5. How to incorporate the prayer board into your daily life?
6. What do I do once the prayer is answered?

Speaker Topics

- How to have the heart of a teacher?
- The Process Through Perversion
- Help! My Heart Needs Deliverance!
- Are We Free In Secret?
- Learning How To Prioritize
- Words Matter: Speak Life
- Dysfunction Between Mothers and Daughters (How to detect it and overcome it?)
- Do Not Be Ensnared By A Title (How to be free with titles?)
- Fruit Flies: What Happens When You Don't Use Your Gifts?
- From Frustration to Forgiveness
- How The Educational System Reflects The Penal System?
- Extreme Rejection for Divine Acceptance
- The Perfect Sin
- Religion and Relationships
- Same Issues Different Interest

- The Cost of The Anointing
- How Sick Are You? Some are physically sick while others are both physically and spiritually sick.

Simene' Walden's Signature Message

Don't Lose ME

(Do Not Lose Your Morals and Ethics In The Marketplace)

The Speech That Quotes

FREE YOURSELF IN YOUR THINKING

Stop following trends and people.
Follow Jesus.
FREE YOURSELF!!

It's a pretty good chance your friend has been running their mouth when someone your friend knows that doesn't know you but yet they don't like you.
FREE YOURSELF of both of them!!

Some secrets ruin relationships while some secrets ruin egos.
FREE YOURSELF!!

Just because God told you to do it doesn't mean you can't still be afraid.
FREE YOURSELF!!

Results can be manipulated.
FREE YOURSELF!!

Don't allow anyone to try and pimp your testimony. You tell it how God wants you to and when he tells you.
FREE YOURSELF!!

Stop trying to include people who want to be excluded.
FREE YOURSELF!!

Stop allowing people to disappoint you. They are not GOD!!
FREE YOURSELF!!

Don't throw up on your supporters.
FREE YOURSELF!!

You will stop getting angry so often with people when you realize how sick they are.
FREE YOURSELF!!

Anyone who doesn't believe in your vision is simply not a part of it. Stop getting upset and
FREE YOURSELF!!

Unhappy people smile in pictures all the time. Smiles aren't indicative of a good life. Some smiles are camouflaged to hide the truth behind the hidden depression that is showing. FREE YOURSELF!!

Some people don't believe they can change so don't expect them to believe that you can.
FREE YOURSELF!!

Don't feel obligated to go around people because it seems like the right thing to do. Do what keeps your heart at ease and your mind at peace.
FREE YOURSELF!!

Watch out for those who will use your name and your story for their promotion but will never promote you.
FREE YOURSELF!!

Not only can you see it, but you can feel division. Just devise a plan to divide yourself from the division.
FREE YOURSELF!!

Don't you allow people to make you feel bad for your accomplishments; small or large. Writing a book is a process and hard work. It's takes lots of time and energy. Don't you allow people who have never written more than a paragraph or page to discourage you from writing the words in your heart in a book. FREE YOURSELF!!

There are some post that you may really like but you don't always click it because others on your page might be offended.
FREE YOURSELF!!

People who refuse to write a paragraph are usually the ones that want to critique your writing. FREE YOURSELF!!

Don't lose your witness over a fool. You become the fool when you do.
FREE YOURSELF!!

Things will never be like they used to be. Every day is a new day.
FREE YOURSELF!!

There are some people who think your event was not successful because they didn't show up. It was much more successful because they didn't show up. FREE YOURSELF!!

Why is the world's gay so unhappy?
FREE YOURSELF!!

It's easier to reject your own when it reminds you of all the times you had the chance but you didn't try. FREE YOURSELF!!

Some people call it blocking on social media. It should be called off cutting off all demonic attachments.
FREE YOURSELF!!

You are not obligated to be attached to anyone that is not attached to your destiny.
FREE YOURSELF!!

Anything that is hindering you, trying to block you, or attempting to sabotage you, get the scissors dipped in red rich blood of Jesus and set in the fire of the Most High God now and severe every demonic tie.
FREE YOURSELF!!

I'd rather smile alone in a picture than to stand beside some haters. FREE YOURSELF!!

When the old memories subtly remind you of all that went wrong, create new memories and FREE YOURSELF!!

Some family members only come around for funerals because the only memory of coming together was when they were killed by the words, actions, and deeds of their family. Death and family are familiar to some only because of it. If that is you
FREE YOURSELF!!

Have you ever been disgusted at the dinner table? Not just by food but by attitudes and behaviors. Nasty attitudes make the food taste worse.
FREE YOURSELF!!

Some people are celebrated and not tolerated where some people are tolerated instead of celebrated. Everyone loves a celebration. Leave the pit and get to the party. FREE YOURSELF!!

If your testimony changes when your environment and the people in it does, you were not convinced and your witness is false.
FREE YOURSELF!!

The battle wounds of believers cut deep.
FREE YOURSELF!!

There is not one person whose way is always right, but it just may be better.
FREE YOURSELF!!

Mean as hell little girls and boys grow up to be mean as hell men and women. Parents set your child free now and then FREE YOURSELF!!

People will talk. You just have to ask the right questions to the right people.
FREE YOURSELF!!

You do not need a large following. You need a loyal following.
FREE YOURSELF!!

You do not need just a shout. You need to be shaken and shifted. FREE YOURSELF!!

Those with the loudest mouths sometimes have the sickest agendas.
FREE YOURSELF!!

There is a process to your progress.
FREE YOURSELF!!

Real friends know your status before you post.
FREE YOURSELF!!

Everyone smiling in pictures are not happy; in fact, some are heavy. Heavy could include emotionally heavy, socially heavy, mentally heavy, spiritually heavy, and sometimes physically heavy. FREE YOURSELF!!

Don't give people the perception of a picture. Give them the reality of who you are.
FREE YOURSELF!!

Anything connected to your demise has to die.
FREE YOURSELF!!

Some people just get along better without being social media friends. If that is you, sometimes the unfriend and not add on social media needs to be applied to all areas of your life.
FREE YOURSELF!!

If you can't make a person feel good, surely don't purposely make them feel bad.
FREE YOURSELF!!

FREE FROM YOUR FAMILY

All families have problems.
FREE YOURSELF!!

Family intimidation and manipulation are the worse.
FREE YOURSELF!!

So what your family knows your secrets. Tell it so you can be free. The worse thing that can happen is if they stopped talking to you. Sometimes the best thing that can happen to you is when someone stops talking to you.
FREE YOURSELF!!

Get the wrong mouth out of your hearing. Make way for God's voice.
FREE YOURSELF!!

The in crowd is really the out crowd.
FREE YOURSELF!!

A poverty mindset says, "Spend on things and never invest in yourself or others".
FREE YOURSELF!!

Don't let anyone prostitute your testimony.
FREE YOURSELF!!

Sometimes people don't want
what we have to offer them.
Sometimes it's just what God told
you to give them.
FREE YOURSELF!!

Your secret will shake up the city.
FREE YOURSELF!!

It is ok to have a family function and not invite all the family.
FREE YOURSELF!!

Take friends with you when you go around family that you do not like. It makes the awkwardness easier.

FREE YOURSELF!!

It is possible to be depressed even spending the holidays with your family. Do not be sucked into tradition and feel obligated to be around people who have ill feelings toward you.
FREE YOURSELF!!

When you become born again you are adopted into a new family. It is ok to spend time with them too. FREE YOURSELF!!

If you had that abortion because your parents told you to, FREE YOURSELF!!

If you were a teenage parent because your boys told you that real men sleep with lots of women,
FREE YOURSELF!!

If you became a young mother because you thought you wanted to have sex with him, but when you told him no, he made you do it anyway,
FREE YOURSELF!!

If your marriage did not work because you learned some things wrong while other things you just didn't know,
FREE YOURSELF!!

Broken men love every other woman except the one they helped create. Daughters, FREE YOURSELF!!

Men who love babies that are not their own while rejecting their mature or adult seed or seeds, do it most of the time because they know a baby cannot yet detect the brokenness in them.
FREE YOURSELF!!

Poverty mindsets can keep families divided.
FREE YOURSELF!!

What happens or happened in this house stays in this house keeps people in bondage. It may not be for everybody but it certainly is for the one who can help you. God has declared he will send you help from His sanctuary. FREE YOURSELF!!

You have the right to safeguard your space from anyone causing you harm.
FREE YOURSELF!!

Stop trying to be spiritually equipped watching religious and bound people.
FREE YOURSELF!!

You can't be a victim and a martyr at the same time. Don't voluntarily offer help and expect compensation for it whether through monetary gain or family accolades.
FREE YOURSELF!!

FREE YOURSELF FROM PEOPLE

It is ok to grieve over the loss of a friendship.
FREE YOURSELF!!

Stop getting offended when someone preaches on your sin and not your neighbors.
FREE YOURSELF!!

Do not go to a dirty hell with a clean house, nice shoes, a pocket or bank account full of money, a super fit body, and a bag. Your guest will enjoy the festivities while you're forever tormented. FREE YOURSELF!!

When you mention the Lord's name, mention it in truth and in righteousness.
FREE YOURSELF!!

The altar is the safest place you can go. Learn how to drop to your knees and surrender.
FREE YOURSELF!!

When you change, people either have to move with the change or be a part of it.
FREE YOURSELF!!

Allow a free person to come back and get you. Bound people are not happy.
FREE YOURSELF!!

Anything that you have built by a foreign god or gods, needs to be destroyed and rebuilt on a new foundation.
FREE YOURSELF!!

Pictures do not mean someone has a relationship with people. It can simply mean people agreed to capture the moment because they were in the same space for a moment in time.
FREE YOURSELF!!

Don't argue with the world. Stand on the Word and
FREE YOURSELF!!

Don't mistake your launching pad for your landing ground. Some people are called to launch you and you are not to land and stay there.
FREE YOURSELF!!

Speak God's Words and not your own. God answers His Word and when it goes out, it will perform that which it was sent to do. Speak God's Words and not your emotions. It does not neglect that your feelings or emotions are not real, they are just not as powerful. FREE YOURSELF!!

Only bound people are mad at you for your freedom.
FREE YOURSELF!!

If you're still wondering why you are not good enough for them this time,
FREE YOURSELF!!

Stop wondering why you're not good enough for them; you're too good for them!
FREE YOURSELF!!

Don't allow the wrong recognition to get you applauds.
FREE YOURSELF!!

Men or women who only make private time for you are really not into you.
FREE YOURSELF!!

Man's agenda and God's agenda will always clash.
FREE YOURSELF!!

A booked calendar or scheduler does not mean God is in it or has approved it.
FREE YOURSELF!!

You can't make people believe in your vision.
FREE YOURSELF!!

Do the work and get the results
for yourself so you can
FREE YOURSELF!!

Stop wanting to be someone else's project and be your own project.
FREE YOURSELF!!

The best thing you can do is
believe in you.
FREE YOURSELF!!

If the voice that is speaking doubt to you more than anyone else is you, stop it and
FREE YOURSELF!!

Don't allow people to give you a deadline and then feel pressure to meet it before time. Their deadline may not be the real deadline. Some people just like things early. FREE YOURSELF!!

If people don't appreciate your genuine private praise, don't go out of your way to give them public praise.
FREE YOURSELF!!

Don't be afraid to say what You believe God is telling you. Sometimes you may be wrong. Other times people will tell you that you are wrong when you're actually right.
FREE YOURSELF!!

The Holy Spirit knows the truth
even when you lie.
FREE YOURSELF!!

You can't convince an insecure person that you believe in them, love them, or want them.
FREE YOURSELF!!

Disagreements do not mean you do not like someone.
FREE YOURSELF!!

Everybody big started off small.
FREE YOURSELF!!

There are some people who love Jesus and never speak about him. I love him so much that's why I speak about him.
FREE YOURSELF!!

Some people love to talk but they don't like to be honest. FREE YOURSELF from such conversations.

There are some women who are still standing after their husbands have broken them because they are standing on the promised God made to them. If you are that woman, FREE YOURSELF of their opinions!!

Don't guard other people hearts out of guilt, fear, or shame.
FREE YOURSELF!!

When you give up your reputation for God, he will give you a new one.
FREE YOURSELF!!

If you have to block your number to call someone you like, you don't need to call them.
FREE YOURSELF!!

The day of the cumulative folder is over. Stop going to others asking about someone or trying to find info about them. Go to them for yourself. Give them a fair chance and make your own decisions based on your interactions with them and how they treat you. The day of the cum folder is over.
FREE YOURSELF!!

Support to be seen is false advertisement.
FREE YOURSELF!!

Stop saying these kids are grown or act grown when you know that the same spirit that attacked you and attached itself to you is that which you see on them manifesting outwardly more bolder than ever. Tell them your story to help free them, and FREE YOURSELF!!

If you don't get help from that which you were a victim of, you can become the victimizer. Stop walking around in shame and full of guilt. FREE YOURSELF!!

Do not desire and own the accessories of this world, yet be headed to hell.
FREE YOURSELF!!

Allow God to override the desires of your flesh so His desires can take precedence in your life.
FREE YOURSELF!!

The Lord knows the things you are into and the things you ought to be into.
FREE YOURSELF!!

People can be nice and wrong.
FREE YOURSELF!!

If a person's post upset you, stop following and friend requesting them.
FREE YOURSELF!!

Fear will keep you at jobs, in careers, in ministries, and in relationships that you want to get out of. FREE YOURSELF!!

Fear is infectious.
FREE YOURSELF!!

Hide in God so he can expose you to people.
FREE YOURSELF!!

Before someone can critique you, make sure they connect and celebrate with you.
FREE YOURSELF!!

If you're rolling with the devil best believe The Student Teacher ain't rolling with you.
FREE YOURSELF!!

Rebuke without relationship is a disaster and an abomination. FREE YOURSELF!!

Everyone wants to make money but in order to make more, you must invest.
FREE YOURSELF!!

Don't lose your witness over a fool.
FREE YOURSELF!!

Don't be more concerned with offending people with God's Word than your own actions and thoughts.
FREE YOURSELF!!

The enemy will liken you to some great person when you are successful. He will liken you to yourself when you fail.
FREE YOURSELF!!

Nasty attitudes while eating make the food taste worse.
FREE YOURSELF!!

FREE YOU FROM YOUR SELF

Shake up the city with your secret.
FREE YOURSELF!!

The problem with media is that some rely on the words of man more than the Words of God. FREE YOURSELF!!

Facebook is not your accountability partner.
FREE YOURSELF!!

Media is not your accountability partner. People who are not accountable to anyone else, especially God, should never be someone you want to hold you accountable.

FREE YOURSELF!!

Those who never take counsel or advice from others is not someone you want to advise you in your life.
FREE YOURSELF!!

Stop looking for people to validate and believe in you who don't even believe in or like you. FREE YOURSELF!!

The most powerful book you can read is the one you read out loud. You are the audio for the book. Read the words and speak your life into existence (Out Loud). This also means be aware of the life you sing, shout, and rap about. You may not want that to manifest.
FREE YOURSELF!!

Stop secretly competing against others. You only wear yourself out. Sadly that person will probably never know that you're trying to beat them so they continue to accomplish their goals and dreams. Why waste energy trying to prove something to someone who doesn't even notice or need your validation?
FREE YOURSELF!!

If you give a gift out of obligation,
you didn't need to give a gift.
FREE YOURSELF!!

If you can't identify if someone is trying to hinder it help you, do yourself a favor and
FREE YOURSELF!!

If your motive is to hinder someone instead of help them, free them and
FREE YOURSELF!!

You can't come up with the come up if all you did was try to bring it down.
FREE YOURSELF!!

You're going to either create the peace you want or the chaos you become or allow in your environment. Choose peace always!
FREE YOURSELF!!

A godly quote a day will keep ignorance, arrogance, and inadequacy away.
FREE YOURSELF!!

The worlds way will get you to the top fast. God's way takes time so he can process you. You have to be strong for that which you have to carry.
FREE YOURSELF!!

Everything is not for everybody.
FREE YOURSELF!!